Dutch Oven Cookbook

Complete Cookbook with Amazing Recipes
Delicious and Easy to Make One Pot Meals

Laura Miller

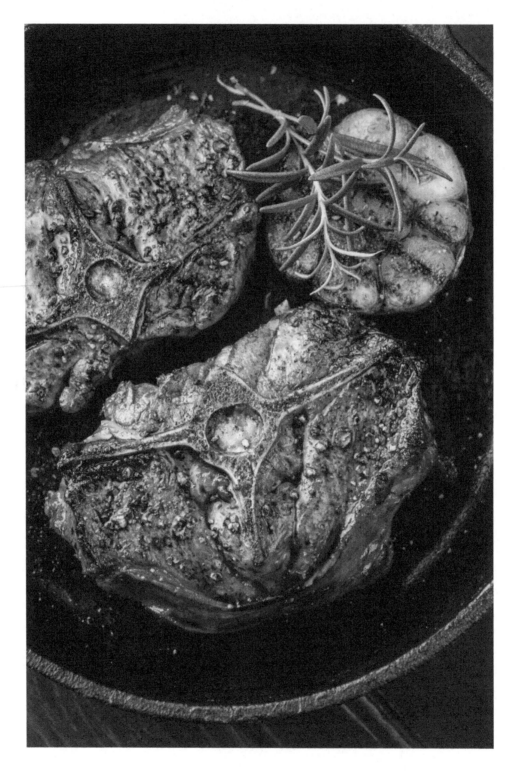

Table of Contents

INTRODUCTION

Dear readers, welcome to this Dutch oven cook book and thank you for making the wise decision of buying this book amongst many other cookbooks to read and learn about the Dutch oven from it. And if you wonder why you should pick this exact cookbook despite the fact that there are tens if not hundreds of similar cookbooks circulating on internet, the response is very easy.

Indeed, I am not intending to repeat the same information documents and data that you are fed up with and I am not just filling pages, in contrast, I am only hoping to clarify the concept of Dutch oven and to offer you some new facts you never heard about this appliance.

Hearing the word Dutch oven and even using it might be a little bit challenging for you, especially if you have never used this cooking appliance before. And on this framework, I am offering you this cookbook entitled "Confessions of a professional Dutch oven Cook, Dutch oven Recipes for your special occasions" and wishing that I can bring you some useful tips that will help properly use the Dutch oven.

So, if you are a beginner to using the Dutch oven, one of the world's most beloved cooking appliances, this Cookbook will prove to you why this appliance has gained unrivalled popularity. You will also discover in this book that the Dutch oven will make the perfect alternative for heavy backpacking ovens that you can use in camping and take it with you wherever you go.

This Dutch Oven Cookbook will also offer you a large array of recipes that will show you how versatile this cooking appliance and why Dutch ovens will make a great addition to your favourite cooking appliances. Besides, the main objective of this Cookbook has been set to provide you with everything you need to know about the Dutch ovens, from its interesting history to its using tips. And through this cookbook, you will get to learn that the pieces known as cast iron Dutch oven makes, by far, one of the most easy-to find and easy-to use cooking appliances. The information you will find in this book will, hopefully, be helpful for all first time as well as professional users alike.

With Dutch oven recipes serving incredible dishes for breakfast, soups, stews, entrees, vegetarian recipes, breads and even desserts, this cookbook will make the best addition to your Book shelf. And this cookbook also provides an overview of everything you need to know about Dutch oven for your everyday use as well as special occasions. In this Dutch oven cookbook, you will also find innovative twists one using Dutch ovens and more. Please don't overlook this book and share it with your friends! Happy Dutch cooking journey!

CHAPTER 1: EVERYTHING YOU SHOULD KNOW ABOUT DUTCH OVEN

DUTCH OVEN, ETYMOLOGY AND HISTORY

The Dutch oven or what is originally referred to as a multi-cooker is a heavy pot that we can use for cooking any of our favourite dishes. Every Dutch oven is equipped with a tight lid and is characterized by thick side walls that are made with cast-iron.

Dutch ovens are known for their ability to retain heat and for its non-sticky nature. This cooking appliance is easy-to use, easy to clean and it doesn't need many sophisticated techniques. Therefore, Dutch ovens make one of the most convenient cooking appliances that we can use in indoor or even outdoor kitchens. Dutch ovens make a perfect choice for camping and it is known for being one of the most versatile cookware appliances that are available in markets. Dutch ovens can be used for roasting, baking, frying, broiling, stewing or steaming.

In a few words, Dutch ovens make the best alternative for conventional ovens and you can use it to cook anything you cook both in oven and stoves. And what makes the Dutch oven wins favour over other backpack ovens is the fact that it takes a very small space in your pack and you can take it with you wherever you go. Dutch oven recipes, usually serves groups of about 6 to 8 people and you can reduce the quantity of food to your liking or you can opt for smaller equipment.

But before starting our Dutch oven cooking journey, let us firs learn a little bit about the origins and history of this unique cooking appliance. For instance, it is said that the invention of the Dutch oven dates back to the year 1492; does this year ring a bell? Indeed, yes, the first Dutch oven ever appeared at the first place, in North America and historians believe that it is Christopher Columbus who brought cast-iron pot with him to the New World. But if the Dutch oven was the discovery of Columbus, why was it referred to as a Dutch invention? Well, Dutch oven originates from the 18th century when Dutch traders sold their cast-iron pots to Indians and New settlers.

The Dutch oven was historically known as a braadpan in the Netherlands and if we seek the exact translation for this word, we can define it as a roasting or frying pan. But the Dutch design that circulates in the market nowadays is an enamelled steel pot that is basically used for frying meats. The modern form of Dutch oven is light and cheap and it is suitable to use with gas and now, we are able to use in indoor kitchens.

And if we look deeper into the history of Dutch ovens, we will discover that this cooking appliance was used in the 17th century and the initial composition of Dutch ovens was mainly cast of brass. The first process of making Dutch ovens consisted of using moulds in order to produce high-quality pots with smooth surfaces while English made it using clay and loam. But as time passed by, the process of making Dutch oven witnessed a great progress and started being used by miners, homesteaders, ranchers and pioneers. And nowadays, we can find a huge variety of Dutch oven brands that spread all over the world.

DUTCH OVEN BENEFITS

Dutch ovens have been used in many countries all over the world for hundreds of years in many culinary traditions. And this cookware was mainly designed to use above open fireplaces and hot coal. Most cast iron Dutch ovens are oven-safe. So what are the benefits and advantages of Dutch ovens?

1. Unlike conventional non-stick cast irons, Dutch ovens are safe and healthy

Not only cast irons are safe-to use, but they are also beneficial and healthy. In fact, using cast irons to prepare your everyday meals will help add a small dietary level of iron to your body. So, with a cast iron, you can make sure that the food you are cooking for your family is one hundred percent safe-to eat.

2. Use Dutch oven if you don't want your food to stick

There is nothing better than a non-stick Dutch oven that brings the taste of the past to your platter and that reminds you of your grandmother's best bread. Dutch ovens are known for its long term of use, you can use it for over thirty years and it will cook in the same way and the same originality.

3. Easy To Clean:

Cleaning kitchen appliances may be one of the most frustrating issues that may frighten a housewife, but not with Dutch ovens. Indeed, Cast irons are characterized by its very easy cleaning process. And when I say Dutch ovens are easy-to clean, I am not saying that we can put it in a dishwasher, of course not, but it can be easily cleaned with a little quantity of hot water. Make sure never to use dish soap to clean a Dutch oven and never use any towels or steel wool because it can damage the Dutch oven. It is recommended to use a sponge instead.

4. Dutch oven is affordable.

Despite the high quality of Dutch ovens, it might be surprising for you that Dutch ovens are extremely affordable and cheaper than many other conventional cooking appliances. And this isn't all, in addition to its affordability, Dutch oven are available everywhere, so you don't have to search hard to find this cooking appliance and you can get it easily with less than 50$.

5. Dutch ovens are highly versatile

Cast iron Dutch ovens are durable, affordable and easy-to find. Besides, this cookware is also versatile. Not only are cast iron Dutch ovens durable, but they are also versatile. They can be used with electric gas, ceramic gas indoors and it can also be used outdoors in campfires or in trips.

6. Using Dutch oven cooks amazingly delicious recipes

If you have a Dutch oven in your house or you found it in your mother's or grandmother's attic and you are thinking of giving it away because you don't know how to use it, it is high time you changed your mind. For instance, you can cook sumptuous dishes in a Dutch oven like cinnamon rolls, fried potatoes and even omelet, bread and many other desserts. If you wonder how the Dutch oven functions, it is very easy; this cookware works as a heat blanket that seals juices and flavours within, which prevents your dishes from drying out.

Important tip:

Whenever you purchase a new cast iron Dutch oven, make sure to purchase it with an oven-safe lid so that you guarantee a safe cooking process.

DUTCH OVEN TIPS

Dutch ovens are credited for being a useful cookware that can last a lifetime, but this can only happen when you follow certain tips that can help you use this cooking appliance properly. And on this note, here are some useful tips you can follow if you want to master the use of Dutch oven:

1. **Whenever you want to use your Dutch oven, make sure to wash it at the first place**

Before you use your Dutch oven for the first time, make sure to wash it with soapy hot water; then dry it with a soft clean cloth. And although many types of Dutch ovens can be washed with the help of a dishwasher, try to hand-wash it instead whenever you can.

2. **Cast iron Dutch oven holds heat very well**

Cast iron Dutch ovens are characterised by its ability to hold heat and thanks to this characteristic, Dutch ovens help retain more heat. Hence, the process of distributing heat during the process of cooking remains balanced allowing more to maintain as many flavours as possible. Besides, the Dutch oven can help keep food warm for quite a long time.

3. **You can use Dutch oven on all heat sources**

You can always use Dutch ovens on top of all heat sources like on a gas stove, in an oven or even in a grill. Besides, Dutch ovens can also work on wood or coal alike. So whenever you are using a Dutch oven, you have the freedom to use whatever heat source you want according to your liking and to the occasion. However, keep in mind to keep the temperature not too hot and not too low either, otherwise, you will risk scorching it.

4. Do never use very high temperatures while using a Dutch oven

When using a Dutch oven, make sure never to use very high temperatures unless you need to boil water, pasta, to reduce the consistency of sauces, stocks or for cooking vegetables. Indeed, Dutch ovens work very well when the heat is balanced and under control; so always make sure never to preheat the Dutch oven on high. Heating a Dutch oven on High can cause your food to stick and believe me you don't want that to happen.

5. Always grease the Dutch oven before using it

As a general rule, you should never cook food in a Dutch oven without greasing it because that way, you are going to risk sticking or burning food. And if you wonder what you can use to grease the Dutch oven with, just use oil, fat or butter.

6. You can marinate ingredients in a Dutch oven

Did you know that you can marinate ingredients in your Dutch oven? Yes, indeed, and don't worry, marinating food in your Dutch oven is a safe option that is safe-to use with raw ingredients or acids.

7. Be careful of scratching your Dutch oven

Whenever you want to use a Dutch oven, be careful of scratching it with a metal and to avoid this risk, it is better to use wooden cooking utensils or silicone. And if you want to avoid the risk of scratching your Dutch oven, avoid any abrasive cleaners like metallic scrubbing pads.

8. Always watch out for the quantity of water you are using

When you want to cook in your Dutch oven, check and double check if necessary to make sure the Dutch oven is dry. And fully dry the Dutch oven when you want to store it on the shelf; also keep it away from the moisture so that the iron won't rust and you end up losing your precious cookware.

9. Pay attention to the cooking timeline

Just about 30 minutes before using your Dutch oven outdoors, you should start a fire. Most Dutch oven meals take about 1 hour to be perfectly cooked. You would want to start the cooking process about two hours before the sunset to have dinner on time.

10. Keep the fire established

Once you have established the campfire for the Dutch oven, keep putting the logs to get a nice coal going. The coal you are going to obtain will help you cook your food properly instead of burning it. It is also recommended to gather some rocks of small size to create a pit. Also be patient and don't open the lid frequently while cooking because you will risk allowing the heat to release and you will eventually delay the cooking process.

Note:

There are many brands and varieties of Dutch ovens, but no matter what type you choose to purchase, you should follow the previous tips in order to make sure your food comes out perfectly cooked. You may also line your Dutch oven with an aluminium foil to help cook better your desserts. And never place the lid on the ground. So are you ready to start this enjoyable cooking journey?

CHAPTER 2: DUTCH OVEN BREAKFAST RECIPES

FRENCH TOAST

(PREP TIME: 2 HOURS | COOK TIME: 1 ½ HOURS | SERVINGS: 8-10)

INGREDIENTS

- 3 Large Granny Smith apples
- 1 Cup of brown sugar
- 1 Medium loaf of French bread
- ½ Cup of butter
- 3 Teaspoons of cinnamon
- ½ Cup of dried cranberries
- 6 Large eggs
- 1 and ½ cups of milk
- 1 Tablespoon of vanilla extract

INSTRUCTIONS

1. Peel the apples, core it then thinly slice it
2. Cut the bread into slices of 1 inch of thickness
3. Heat the Dutch oven to a temperature of about 225 degrees over coals to attain simmering
4. Melt the butter in your Dutch oven.
5. Stir in the brown sugar and about 1 teaspoon of cinnamon.
6. Remove the Dutch oven from the heat; then stir in the apples and the cranberries and press so that you have a flat surface
7. Lay the slices of white bread over the top with the cut side up in a way that you make 1 filled layer
8. Beat the eggs and pour in the milk, the vanilla, and about 2 teaspoons of cinnamon.
9. Pour the egg mixture over the bread.
10. Cover the Dutch over with a lid and set aside to let the bread soak for about 1 hour or for an overnight
11. Bake the French toast for about 60 minutes
12. When ready, flip the French toast upside down over a plate
13. Serve and enjoy your breakfast!

NUTRITION INFORMATION

Calories: 379, Fat: 15.1g, Carbohydrates: 36g, Protein: 12.3g, Dietary Fiber 1.8 g

FLUFFY PANCAKES

(PREP TIME: 8 MINUTES | COOK TIME: 30 MINUTES | SERVINGS: 3-4)

INGREDIENTS

- 3 Large eggs
- ½ Cup of flour
- ½ Cup of milk
- 1 Tablespoon of sugar
- 1 Pinch of nutmeg
- 4 Tablespoons of butter
- 2 Tablespoons of maple Syrup

INSTRUCTIONS

1. Preheat an oven to a temperature of 425 degrees.
2. Combine the eggs with the flour, the milk, the sugar and the nutmeg into a blender jar and mix very well until you get a smooth batter or you can just do it manually
3. Place the butter in a heavy cast-iron Dutch oven of about 10 inches
4. Put the cast iron Dutch oven in the oven and let the butter melt for a couple of minutes
5. Remove the cast iron Dutch oven from the oven and pour in the batter
6. Return the cast iron Dutch oven to the oven and bake for about 20 minutes at a temperature of about 300° F
7. Remove the pancake from the oven and cut it into wedges

8. Top with confectioners 'sugar or with cinnamon sugar
9. Serve and enjoy your breakfast!

NUTRITION INFORMATION

Calories: 298, Fat: 19.2g, Carbohydrates: 18.2g, Protein: 12.6g, Dietary Fiber 0.5 g

OVEN BAKED DUTCH OVEN CHEESY SWEET POTATOES

(PREP TIME: 15 MINUTES | COOK TIME: 45 MINUTES | SERVINGS: 8-10)

INGREDIENTS

- 8 Large sweet potatoes
- 1 lb of cooked and crumbled thick sliced bacon
- 2 Cups of shredded cheese
- 1 Cup of sliced onions
- 1 Pinch of salt
- 1 Pinch of pepper to taste

INSTRUCTIONS

1. Start by slicing the potatoes into thin slices; then slice the onion into rings and set aside
2. Cut the bacon into strips; then into pieces of 1 inch each
3. Heat up the Dutch oven on top of hot coals, stove or grill; then fry the bacon until it gets crispy texture
4. Remove the bacon, but don't remove the grease from the bottom of the Dutch oven
5. Now, start making layers and place 1 layer of potatoes, the sliced onions, the bacon and the cheese
6. Repeat the same layers; then Cover your Dutch oven with a lid and cook for about 45 minutes at a temperature of about 375° F
7. Remove from the oven; then serve and enjoy your breakfast!

NUTRITION INFORMATION

Calories: 358, Fat: 24.6g, Carbohydrates: 23g, Protein: 10.52g, Dietary Fiber: 2.1 g

BREAKFAST PIZZA

(PREP TIME: 20 MINUTES | COOK TIME: 35 MINUTES | SERVINGS: 6)

INGREDIENTS

- 6 Crumbled strips of Bacon
- ½ Pound of crumbled Breakfast Sausage
- 1 Minced garlic clover
- ½ Chopped green Bell Pepper
- ½ Chopped red Bell Pepper
- ½ Chopped, Onion
- 5 Sliced Mushrooms
- 1 Tube of Refrigerator Crescent Rolls
- 6 Beaten eggs
- 1 Teaspoon of Italian Seasoning
- ½ Teaspoon of Red Pepper Flakes
- 1 Pinch of Salt
- 1 Pinch of pepper
- 1 Cup of shredded Mozzarella Cheese
- 1 Cup of Shredded Cheddar Cheese

INSTRUCTIONS

1. Spray the Dutch oven with a non-stick cooking spray or just line your Dutch oven with a tin foil and spray it with cooking spray
2. Cook the bacon; then drain the grease and set it aside to cool and crumble it once it is cooked
3. Brown the sausage; then drain the grease and mix in the garlic, the peppers, the onions and the mushrooms and sauté for about 4 to 5 minutes
4. Remove the mixture from the heat and set it aside
5. Unroll the crescent rolls in the Dutch oven and line the base with it; then make the crust of the pizza by pinching your dough along the side of your Dutch oven up to about 1 inch
6. Fill your crust with the meat and the veggie mixture; then add in the Italian seasoning, the red pepper, the salt and the ground black pepper
7. Pour the meat and the veggies mixture; then sprinkle the cheese on top and cover your Dutch oven with a lid and place it on a fire
8. Bake your pizza for about 25 to 30 minutes
9. Remove from the heat; then let your pizza cool for about a few minutes
10. Slice your pizza; then serve and enjoy it!

NUTRITION INFORMATION

Calories: 309, Fat: 11.6g, Carbohydrates: 25g, Protein: 21.5g, Dietary Fiber: 2.5g

CHAPTER 3: DUTCH OVEN STEWS AND SOUPS

CREAMY MEAT STEW

(PREP TIME: 15 MINUTES | COOK TIME: 2 ½ HOURS | SERVINGS: 4)

INGREDIENTS

- 1 lb of stew meat
- 1 sliced onion
- 3 carrots, chopped
- 1 can of 15 oz of chopped tomatoes
- 12 Oz of beef broth
- 8 oz of tomato sauce
- 1/3 cup of flour
- 1 tsp of garlic salt
- 1 tbsp of Worcestershire sauce
- 1 ½ lbs of quartered baby red potatoes
- 2 Cups of halved mushrooms
- ½ Teaspoon of oregano
- ½ Teaspoon of salt

INSTRUCTIONS

1. Put the stew meat in your Dutch oven; then add the onions, the carrots, the salt, the oregano, the sauce and the diced tomatoes
2. Pour in the beef broth over the top and make sure all the veggies are also coated
3. Mix the flour with the tomato sauce in a bowl; then pour it on top in your Dutch oven and stir
4. Cover the Dutch oven with a lid and place it in a preheated oven to a temperature of about 350° F for about 90 minutes
5. Remove the Dutch oven from the oven and add the chopped potatoes, then cover with a lid and cook for about 90 additional minutes
6. Serve and enjoy your stew!

NUTRITION INFORMATION

Calories: 277, Fat: 6g, Carbohydrates: 28g, Protein: 25g, Dietary Fiber 3.9 g

CLAM CHOWDER

(PREP TIME: 12 MINUTES | COOK TIME: 20MINUTES | SERVINGS: 3-4)

INGREDIENTS

- 4 Bacon strips, centre-cut
- 2 Chopped celery ribs
- 1 Large, chopped onion
- 1 Minced garlic clove
- 3 Small, peeled and diced potatoes
- 1 Cup of water
- 1 Bottle of 8 ounces of clam juice
- 3 Teaspoons of reduced-sodium chicken bouillon granules
- ¼ Teaspoon of white pepper
- ¼ Teaspoon of dried thyme
- 1/3 Cup of all-purpose flour
- 2 Cups of fat-free half-and-half, divided
- 2 Cans of about 6 ounces of undrained, chopped clams

INSTRUCTIONS

1. In your Dutch oven, cook the bacon over a medium heat until it becomes crispy.
2. Remove the bacon to paper towels and let drain; then set aside and sauté the celery and the onion until it becomes tender
3. Add the garlic and cook for about 1 minute; then add in the potatoes, the water, the bouillon, the pepper, the clam juice, the thyme and the pepper and bring the mixture to a boil for about 15 to 20 minutes
4. In a medium bowl, mix the flour with 1 cup of the half-and-half and mix; then add the mixture to the Dutch oven gradually and cook while stirring for about 2 minutes
5. Stir in the clams and the remaining quantity of half-and-half and heat, but don't boil anymore
6. Top with the crumbled bacon and ladle the soup into bowls
7. Serve and enjoy your soup!

NUTRITION INFORMATION

Calories: 260, Fat: 4g, Carbohydrates: 9g, Protein: 13g, Dietary Fiber: 3g

HOBO STEW

INGREDIENTS

- 1 tablespoon of olive oil
- 1 Small, chopped onion
- ½ Cup of hot and sweet peppers, chopped
- ½ Cup of chopped celery
- 1 Tablespoon of finely minced garlic
- 1 and ½ pounds of finely ground beef
- 2 ½ tablespoons of all purpose flour
- 1 and ½ cups of beef broth
- 3 Cans of about 11.5 ounces each of tomato juice
- 1 Can of 14.5 ounces of chopped tomatoes
- 2 Large, peeled and chopped potatoes
- 2 Large chopped tomatoes
- 2 Heap cups of corn
- 2 Cups of green beans, chopped
- 1 Dash of Worcestershire sauce
- ¼ Cup of hot sauce
- Couple dashes of hot sauce
- 1/4 Teaspoon of seasoning, Cajun seasoning or Italian seasoning
- 1 Teaspoon of salt, kosher
- ¼ Teaspoon of freshly ground black pepper

INSTRUCTIONS

1. Start by heating the olive oil in the bottom of a Dutch oven over a medium heat
2. Add in the onion, the peppers and the celery; then cook and stir until the mixture is softened for about 3 minutes
3. Add the garlic and the ground beef and brown for about 5 minutes
4. Drain any excess of fats and sprinkle the meat with the flour and cook while stirring for about 3 minutes
5. Pour in the beef stock and the diced tomatoes.
6. Add in the carrots, the potatoes, the corn and the green beans
7. Add the Worcestershire hot sauce and the seasonings and stir; the cover and cover the Dutch oven with a lid
8. Let simmer over a medium low heat for about 2 hours
9. Serve and enjoy your hobo stew!

NUTRITION INFORMATION

Calories: 241, Fat: 13.8g, Carbohydrates: 17g, Protein: 12.5g, Dietary Fiber: 2.4g

BEEF AND ONION SOUP

(PREP TIME: 10 MINUTES | COOK TIME: 45 HOURS |
SERVINGS: 3)

INGREDIENTS

- 5 Medium, thinly sliced onions
- ½ Pound of beef steak
- 2 Tablespoons of olive oil
- 3 Sprigs of fresh thyme
- 1 Pinch of Black pepper
- 5 Cups of beef broth
- 1 Tablespoon of tomato paste
- 1 and ½ cups of beef stock

INSTRUCTIONS

1. In your Dutch oven and over a medium heat on the stove; heat the oil; then add the onion and the thyme and sauté for 3 minutes
2. Cut the beef meat into small cubes; then add it to the Dutch oven
3. Brown the meat for about 5 minutes; then add 1 cup of the beef stock
4. Cover the Dutch oven and cook for about 40 minutes, you can stir from time to time
5. Add the tomato paste and the remaining quantity of the stock and recover with the lid
6. Let simmer for about 5 minutes
7. Remove the Dutch oven from the heat; then garnish with finely sliced parsley
8. Serve and enjoy your soup!

NUTRITION INFORMATION

Calories: 165, Fat: 6.3g, Carbohydrates: 14.5g, Protein: 14.85g, Dietary Fiber: 1.5g

BUTTER SQUASH SOUP

(PREP TIME: 7 MINUTES | COOK TIME: 30 MINUTES | SERVINGS: 3-4)

INGREDIENTS

- 2 Pounds of peeled and diced Butternut Squash
- 3 Tablespoons of olive oil
- 1 Large, chopped onion
- 2 Pounds of beef steak
- 32Oz of Beef Stock
- 2 Smashed garlic cloves
- Fresh sprig of thyme
- 1 Sprig of fresh rosemary
- 1 Teaspoon of salt
- 1 Teaspoon of pepper

INSTRUCTIONS

1. Peel the squash and chop it into small dices; make sure to remove the seeds
2. Pour the olive oil into a large Dutch oven and over a medium high heat
3. Add in the onion and sauté it for about 2 to 3 minutes
4. Pour in the beef stock, the herbs, the salt and the pepper
5. Cover your Dutch oven with a lid and cook in over a medium low heat for about 30 minutes
6. Remove the lid and top your soup with parsley
7. Remove the Dutch oven from the heat
8. Puree your soup with a blender
9. Ladle the soup in serving bowls of your choice
10. Serve and enjoy your nutritious squash soup!

NUTRITION INFORMATION

Calories: 281, Fat: 7.9g, Carbohydrates: 6.8g, Protein: 15.5g, Dietary Fiber: 2g

CHAPTER 4: DUTCH OVEN MEAT RECIPES

DUTCH OVEN BEEF ROAST

(PREP TIME: 20 MINUTES | COOK TIME: 2 HOURS | SERVINGS: 5)

INGREDIENTS

- 2 tablespoons of olive oil
- 1 small, finely sliced red onion
- 2 Pounds of chuck roast
- 1 teaspoon of salt
- 1/2 teaspoon of black pepper
- 4 Cups of beef broth
- 3 Peeled and sliced Large sweet or russet potatoes
- 5 Peeled and sliced into pieces of 1 inch of thickness carrots

INSTRUCTIONS

1. Preheat your oven to a temperature of about 375° F.
2. Put the Dutch oven on top of the stove and set the heat to high for about 5 minutes; the sear the meat; add the oil and season the beef meat with the salt and pepper on all sides
3. Add the meat to the Dutch oven and sear for about 4 minutes; then flip and add the onions
4. Cook for about 5 minutes; then add the beef broth and cover the Dutch oven with its lid
5. Bake for about 1 and ½ hours; then check if there is enough liquid, if not, you can add 1 additional cup of water
6. Lower the heat to 350° F and bake for 1 additional hour; then add the potatoes and the carrots and bake for about 45 minutes
7. Serve and enjoy your dish!

NUTRITION INFORMATION

Calories: 500, Fat: 18g, Carbohydrates: 13g, Protein: 24g, Dietary Fiber: 1.2g

OSSO BUCO

INGREDIENTS

- 5 cuts of veal shanks
- 1 Teaspoon of kosher salt
- ¾ Teaspoon of ground black pepper
- 2 Tablespoons of Dijon mustard
- 1 Cup of all-purpose flour
- 2 Tablespoons of butter or duck fat
- 2 Finely minced shallots
- 1 Finely minced carrot
- 12 Finely minced garlic cloves
- 1 tablespoon of red curry paste
- ⅛ Teaspoon of caraway seeds
- 1 Cup of red wine
- 2½ cups of beef stock
- 3 Sprigs of fresh thyme
- Pita or crusty bread for serving

INSTRUCTIONS

1. Start by preheating your oven to about 325 degrees F; then dry the veal shanks with paper towels and tie each with a twine around it
2. Rub the meat shanks with 1 pinch of salt and 1 pinch of pepper; then rub it with the Dijon Mustard
3. Add in the duck fat and the Dijon mustard. Then dredge the meat shanks in the flour and set it aside
4. Add the duck fat to a Dutch pan over a medium high heat on the stove top
5. Place the veal in the Dutch oven and sear it on all sides for around 4 minutes; then transfer the seared meat to a plate and set it aside
6. Add 1 additional tablespoon of butter or duck fat; then add in the shallots and the carrots and stir for about 5 minutes over a medium high heat
7. Add the garlic and cook for about 2 minutes
8. Add in the wine, the stock and the curry paste; then return the meat back to the Dutch oven and add some sprigs of thyme.
9. Cover your Dutch oven with a lid and place the Dutch oven in an oven at a temperature of about 325° F and bake for about 2 ½ hours
10. Serve and enjoy your dish with the crusty bread!

NUTRITION INFORMATION

Calories: 444, Fat: 10g, Carbohydrates: 11.3g, Protein: 57g, Dietary Fiber: 2.8g

HABANERO BEEF WITH POMEGRANATE JUICE

(PREP TIME: 15 MINUTES | COOK TIME: 3 HOURS | SERVINGS: 6)

INGREDIENTS

- 2 Pounds of beef chuck roast
- 2 Teaspoon of fine sea salt
- 1 Tablespoon of ghee
- 1 Seeded and finely chopped large jalapeño pepper
- 2Cups of reduced sodium beef broth
- 2 Cups of pomegranate juice
- 1 Pinch of sea salt
- 1 Pinch of black pepper

INSTRUCTIONS

1. Preheat your oven to a temperature of about 325°F
2. Pat your meat roast dry with the help of paper towels; then season it with salt
3. In a Dutch oven and over a medium heat; pour in the ghee
4. Sear the meat on all its sides for around 5 minutes
5. Add the jalapeno, the beef broth and the pomegranate juice; then close the lid of the Dutch oven
6. Sprinkle the pomegranate arils over the steak
7. Place the Dutch oven and place the pot into your oven
8. Bake your meal for about 3 hours
9. Once the meat is perfectly cooked; remove the pot from the oven; then shred it with a fork
10. Now, prepare the pomegranate juice by boiling it into a small pan over a low heat
11. Serve and enjoy your lunch!

NUTRITION INFORMATION

Calories: 164.9, Fat: 5.7g, Carbohydrates: 13.6g, Protein: 15.4g, Dietary Fiber: 1.7 g

GROUND BEEF BOBOTIE

(PREP TIME: 10 MINUTES | COOK TIME: 40 MINUTES | SERVINGS: 5)

INGREDIENTS

- 1 and ½ pounds of ground beef
- 2 Slices of soaked bread
- 2 Medium and chopped onions
- 1 Tablespoon of chutney
- 2 Teaspoons of ground curry powder
- 4 Teaspoons of ground turmeric
- ½ Teaspoon of salt
- 2 Whole bay leaves
- 1 Beaten egg
- 1 Cup of almond milk
- 1 Tablespoon of avocado oil
- Coconut for garnishing

INSTRUCTIONS

1. Preheat your oven to a temperature of about 340° F
2. In a large wok and over a medium heat on top of a stove, put the turmeric and the curry; then allow the flavours to mix up for about 2 minutes
3. Add in the chutney and cook for about 2 minutes
4. Add the ketchup and cook your ingredients for 1 additional minute.
5. Strain the water from your bread; then keep stirring
6. Add the meat and stir it with a fork
7. Add the salt and the bay leaves; then cook it for several minutes
8. Remove the bay leaves
9. Place the mixture of the Bobotie meat into a greased Dutch oven
10. Make the topping by beating the egg with the milk
11. Pour the mixture of the egg and the milk into the Dutch oven
12. Place the Dutch oven in your oven and bake the Bobotie for about 40 minutes
13. Remove the Bobotie from the oven; then set it aside to cool for several minutes
14. Serve and enjoy your flavourful Bobotie!

NUTRITION INFORMATION

Calories: 342, Fat: 16.87g, Carbohydrates: 16g, Protein: 27.5g, Dietary Fiber: 1.5 g

EGGPLANT LAMB CURRY

INGREDIENTS

- 1½ Pounds of peeled eggplant
- 3 Pound of trimmed lamb shanks
- 2 Tablespoons of ground sumac, divided
- 1¼ Teaspoons of salt
- ½ Teaspoon of freshly ground pepper
- 2 Tablespoons of extra-virgin olive oil, divided
- 1 Diced green bell pepper
- 1 Small onion
- 3 Finely chopped garlic cloves
- 5 Chopped plum tomatoes
- 1 Cup of water
- ½ Cup of finely chopped parsley, divided

INSTRUCTIONS

1. Slice the eggplant into slices of ½ inch each lengthwise; then slice crosswise into pieces of 1 inch each and set aside
2. Heat about 1 tablespoon of oil in a large Dutch oven over a medium-high heat.
3. Add in the lamb and cook for about 5 to 7 minutes and transfer to a plate
4. Add the remaining quantity of oil to a Dutch oven; then add the bell pepper, the onion, garlic and 1 tablespoon of sumac.
5. Cook while stirring for about 4 minutes; then return the lamb to the Dutch oven and add in the eggplant, the tomatoes and the water and let boil for 3 minutes
6. Return the lamb shanks to the Dutch oven; and bring the mixture to a boil on a medium low heat
7. Cover the Dutch oven with a lid and cook for 2 hours. Remove the lamb meat to a serving plate and cover with foil to keep it warm
8. Increase the heat and let the sauce thicken for 6 minutes
9. Remove the Dutch oven off the heat and stir in about ¼ cup of parsley; then combine the remaining quantity of parsley with the remaining quantity of garlic in a bowl
10. Serve with your dish with the lamb and the vegetable sauce!

NUTRITION INFORMATION

Calories: 321, Fat: 14g, Carbohydrates: 20g, Protein: 35g, Dietary Fiber: 4 g

CHAPTER 5: DUTCH OVEN POULTRY RECIPES

SPICY CHICKEN THIGHS WITH FENNEL

(PREP TIME: 10 MINUTES | COOK TIME: 65 MINUTES | SERVINGS: 8)

INGREDIENTS

- 8 Skin on and bon in chicken thighs about 3 and ½ pounds
- 1 Pinch of salt
- 1 Pinch of pepper
- ½ Teaspoon of red pepper flakes
- 6 Minced garlic cloves
- ½ Teaspoon of crushed fennel seeds
- 1 Tablespoon of finely chopped rosemary
- 1 Tablespoon of olive oil
- 2 Lemons, cut into wedges
- 1 Cup of green and black olives with pits
- 1 Cup of chicken broth
- 3 Tablespoons of chopped parsley

INSTRUCTIONS

1. Start by patting the chicken thighs dry with the help of paper towels.
2. Season your chicken meat very well with 1 generous pinch of salt and 1 pinch of black pepper
3. Put the chicken in a large Dutch oven with the skin on the upside
4. Sprinkle a little bit of red pepper; fennel, garlic and rosemary; then drizzle all together with the olive oil
5. Rub the seasoning into the chicken thighs and tuck the lemon wedges within the meat
6. Set the chicken aside to marinade for about 15 minutes
7. Heat the oven to about 375° F and put the Dutch oven in the preheated oven
8. Bake the chicken for about 20 minutes
9. After the 20 minutes, add the olives to the tray and the chicken broth
10. Cook the chicken-olive mixture for about 45 minutes
11. Remove the chicken and the lemon wedges; then arrange it over a platter
12. Serve your chicken with parsley for garnish
13. Enjoy!

NUTRITION INFORMATION

Calories: 156, Fat: 12.3g, Carbohydrates: 2g, Protein: 33.9g, Dietary Fiber: 1 g

CHICKEN WITH PROSCIUTTO AND OLIVES

(PREP TIME: 8 MINUTES | COOK TIME: 60 MINUTES | SERVINGS: 6-7)

INGREDIENTS

- 6 to 7 chicken thighs
- 1 Tablespoon of Coconut oil
- 1 Finely shallot
- 1 Teaspoon of minced garlic
- 2 Cups of squeezed and frozen Spinach
- 5 Roughly chopped Artichoke hearts
- 1/3 Cup of chopped Kalamata olives
- 1 Pinch of taste
- 1 Pinch of pepper
- 6 slices of Prosciutto
- 1 Drizzle of Olive oil

INSTRUCTIONS

1. Preheat your oven to about 325° F
2. Remove any excess of fat off the chicken thighs; then heat the oil into a large frying wok over a medium heat
3. Add the garlic and the shallots; then stir until it becomes fragrant for about 2 minutes
4. Add the spinach, the artichoke hearts, and the olives
5. Mix very well and cook your ingredients for about 4 minutes
6. Remove from the heat and set the ingredients aside into a small bowl
7. Now, time to scoop the veggie mixture in the chicken thighs; then wrap it
8. Wrap each of the chicken thighs together with a prosciutto slice; then hold the prosciutto with the use of tooth
9. Drizzle a little bit of olive oil into a Dutch oven
10. Place the wrapped chicken thighs into the Dutch oven and cover it with the lid
11. Bake the chicken for about 55 minutes at a temperature of about 350° F
12. Serve and enjoy your dish!

NUTRITION INFORMATION

Calories: 290.1, Fat: 13.2g, Carbohydrates: 1.3g, Protein: 36g, Dietary Fiber: 1.3 g

TANGY CHICKEN WITH PINEAPPLE AND PEACH PUREE

(PREP TIME: 8 MINUTES | COOK TIME: 45 MINUTES | SERVINGS: 5)

INGREDIENTS

- 2 and ½ pounds of chicken breast
- 1 Can crushed pineapple
- 1 Large juiced orange
- ½ Cup of raisins
- ½ Cup of sliced almonds
- ¼ Teaspoon of cinnamon
- ¼ Teaspoon of ground cloves
- ¼ Teaspoon of freshly ground black pepper
- 3 Medium pureed and fresh or frozen sliced peaches

INSTRUCTIONS

1. Cut the chicken to your liking
2. In a large Dutch oven, combine the chicken with the pineapple; the orange juice, the raisins, the almonds, the cinnamon and the cloves
3. Place the Dutch oven over a medium high heat and cover it with the lid; then let your ingredients, simmer for about 45 minutes, you can flip from time to time
4. Add the peach puree and let simmer with the rest of the ingredients uncovered for about 15 minutes
5. When the chicken sauce gets the thickness you like, season it with a little bit of fresh black pepper
6. Serve and enjoy!

NUTRITION INFORMATION

Calories: 290.1, Fat: 13.2g, Carbohydrates: 1.3g, Protein: 36g, Dietary Fiber: 1.3 g

CHICKEN ADOBO

(PREP TIME: 10 MINUTES | COOK TIME: 55 MINUTES | SERVINGS: 4-5)

INGREDIENTS

- 1 and ½ pounds of cubed skin-on boneless chicken thighs
- ¼ Cup and 2 tablespoons of apple cider vinegar
- ¼ Cup of coconut aminos
- 1 to 2 dried bay leaves
- ½ Teaspoons of coarse ground black pepper
- 1 Pinch of sea salt
- 2 Tablespoons of coconut oil
- 4 Hardboiled, peeled large eggs

INSTRUCTIONS

1. Add the chicken thighs to a large Dutch oven and pour the cider on top
2. Add the coconut aminos, the bay leaves and the black pepper.
3. Place the Dutch oven over a low heat and cover with a lid; then let simmer for about 30 minutes
4. Season the chicken with the salt and let simmer for about 10 minutes
5. Remove the chicken and the sauce from the Dutch oven and set it aside
6. Pour in the coconut oil and add to it the chicken meat; sauté altogether for about 5 minutes
7. Add the hardboiled eggs and pour the sauce over it; then mix the ingredients for the egg to be coated very well
8. Let the ingredients simmer for about 10 minutes
9. Serve and enjoy your Chicken adobo!

NUTRITION INFORMATION

Calories: 174, Fat: 5g, Carbohydrates: 0.9g, Protein: 22g, Dietary Fiber: 4 g

TURKEY LIVERS WITH HERBS

(PREP TIME: 5 MINUTES | COOK TIME: 30 MINUTES | SERVINGS: 3-4)

INGREDIENTS

- 2 Tablespoons of olive oil
- 2 Minced garlic cloves
- ½ Pound of organic turkey livers
- 1 and ½ tablespoons of arrowroot powder or of almond meal
- ¼ Teaspoon of unprocessed salt
- 2 Tablespoons of chopped fresh herbs like thyme
- The Zest of 1 lemon
- 3 Tablespoons of lemon juice
- 4 Chopped anchovy fillets
- 3 Tablespoons of filtered water
- Chopped herbs and lemon wedges for garnish
- 1 ½ cups of chicken stock

INSTRUCTIONS

1. Heat the oil into a large Dutch oven wok over a medium heat
2. Add in the garlic and sprinkle the turkey with the almond meal and the arrowroot
3. Put the turkey livers into the heated Dutch oven and sear it for about 2 minutes
4. Add the salt, the herb, the zest, the lemon, the juice and the anchovies
5. Stir your ingredients; then pour in 1 and ½ cups of chicken stock
6. Cover the Dutch oven with a lid and let simmer for about 20 to 25 minutes
7. Top your dish with chopped parsley
8. Serve and enjoy your dish!

NUTRITION INFORMATION

Calories: 115, Fat: 2g, Carbohydrates: 2g, Protein: 18g, Dietary Fiber: 2.1 g

CHAPTER 6: DUTCH OVEN FISH RECIPES

SALMON WITH CAPERS AND LIME

(PREP TIME: 10 MINUTES | COOK TIME: 35 MINUTES | SERVINGS: 4)

INGREDIENTS

- 4 Salmon fillets
- The juice of 1 lemon or lime
- ½ Cup of extra virgin olive oil
- ½ Cup of unsalted avocado oil
- 2 Thinly sliced shallots
- 3 Thinly sliced garlic cloves
- 2 Tablespoons of capers
- 1 Teaspoon of seasoned salt
- Teaspoon of ground black pepper
- 1 Teaspoon of ground cumin
- 1Teaspoon of garlic powder
- 1 and ½ pounds of flounder
- 5 Trimmed green onions from the top; cut the onion lengthwise
- 1 Sliced lime or lemon
- ¾ Cup of chopped fresh dill

INSTRUCTIONS

1. In a small bowl, mix altogether the olive oil with the avocado oil

2. Season with a little bit of the seasoned salt and add the shallots, the garlic and the capers.

3. In a separate bowl; mix the seasoned salt with the pepper, the cumin and the garlic powder.

4. Spice the salmon fillets, each on both sides.

5. Put the salmon fillets into a greased Dutch oven; then cover with the mixture of lemon that you have already prepared.

6. Arrange the onion halves and the limes right on top

7. Cover the Dutch oven with its lid and place it in a preheated Dutch oven

8. Bake the salmon for about 25 to 30 minutes at a temperature of 375° F

9. Remove the salmon from the oven and garnish with chopped fresh dill

10. Serve and enjoy your Dutch oven baked salmon with a salad of your choice and enjoy!

NUTRITION INFORMATION

Calories: 142, Fat: 4g, Carbohydrates: 3g, Protein: 24.6g, Dietary Fiber: 0.8 g

GNOCCHI WITH SALMON

(PREP TIME: 5 MINUTES | COOK TIME: 23 MINUTES | SERVINGS: 5)

INGREDIENTS

- 2 Tablespoons of olive oil
- 1 Finely sliced onion, finely sliced
- 1 Head of broccoli, separated into small florets
- 2 Cups of reduced-fat cream cheese
- 3 Tablespoons of fresh pesto
- 1 Pound of fresh gnocchi
- The Juice 1 lemon
- 4 Organic salmon fillets

INSTRUCTIONS

1. Start by heating the oven to a temperature of about 375° F
2. Heat the olive oil in large Dutch oven over a medium high heat on top of a stove; sauté the onion for about 3 minutes; then add in the broccoli and cook for about 2 minutes
3. Add in the cream cheese, the pesto and about 100ml of water; then heat the mixture gently, while stirring from time to time
4. In the meantime; microwave the gnocchi for about 1 minute or cook it according to the package instructions
5. Add the gnocchi to the Dutch oven and season with the black pepper, then salt and lemon juice
6. Place the salmon fillets into the Dutch oven and cover with a lid
7. Transfer the Dutch oven to the preheated oven and bake for about 20 minutes
8. Serve and enjoy your dish right away!

NUTRITION INFORMATION

Calories: 244.9, Fat: 16.7g, Carbohydrates: 13.2g, Protein: 9.5g, Dietary Fiber: 1 g

COD FISH WITH TOMATO SAUCE AND HERBS

(PREP TIME: 10 MINUTES | COOK TIME: 25 MINUTES | SERVINGS: 3)

INGREDIENTS

- To make the Tomato Basil Sauce:
- 2 Tablespoons of olive oil
- ½ Teaspoon of crushed red pepper flakes
- 2 Large, finely minced garlic cloves
- 1 Sliced pint of cherry tomatoes
- ¼ Cup of dry white wine
- ½ Cup of finely chopped fresh basil
- 2 Tablespoons of fresh lemon juice
- ½ Teaspoon of fresh lemon zest
- ½ Teaspoon of salt
- ¼ Teaspoon of fresh ground black pepper
- To prepare the Cod:
- 2 Tablespoons of olive oil
- 1 and ½ pounds of fresh and cut cod
- 1 Pinch of salt and 1 pinch of pepper

INSTRUCTIONS

FOR THE WHITE WINE TOMATO BASIL SAUCE

1. Heat the oil in a large Dutch oven over a medium high heat
2. Add the crushed red pepper flakes and the garlic; then sauté the ingredients altogether for about 2 to 3 minutes
3. Add the tomatoes and cook the ingredients for about 15 minutes; but make sure to stir from time to time
4. Pour in the white wine and let simmer; then add the basil, the lemon juice, the lemon zest, the salt and the pepper and cook for about 5 minutes
5. Transfer your sauce to a medium bowl; then set it aside

FOR THE COD

6. Clean the Dutch oven and heat the oil in it
7. Season both the sides of the Cod with the salt and the pepper.
8. Put the cod into the oil and cook it for about 4 minutes
9. Flip the cod from time to time and bake it in the oven for about 5 minutes
10. Pour the wine over the tomato basil sauce and serve it.
11. Enjoy your dish!

NUTRITION INFORMATION

Calories: 163.4, Fat: 4.3g, Carbohydrates: 4.4g, Protein: 21g, Dietary Fiber: 0.8 g

SPICY FISH WITH POTATOES

(PREP TIME: 5 MINUTES | COOK TIME: 35 MINUTES | SERVINGS: 4-5)

INGREDIENTS

- 1 Tablespoon of paprika
- 1 Tablespoon of smoked paprika
- ½ Teaspoon of cumin
- ½ Teaspoon of oregano
- ½ Teaspoon of garlic powder
- ½ Teaspoon of salt
- ¼ Teaspoon of coriander
- ¼ Teaspoon of black pepper
- 1/8 Teaspoon of cayenne pepper
- 1 Tablespoon of olive oil
- 4 Chopped potatoes
- 1 and ½ pounds of cod filets
- 1 Chopped zucchini
- 1 Chopped summer squash
- 6 Oz of fish
- 1 and ½ cups of veggies

INSTRUCTIONS

1. Preheat your oven to about 400° F.
2. Mix your ingredients together with the spices in order to create the seasoning
3. Add the sweet potatoes with the olive oil and with half of the seasoning mixture
4. Line the Dutch oven with aluminium foil and grease it with cooking spray
5. Arrange the potatoes in the bottom of the Dutch oven and cover with a lid
6. Bake the fish and potatoes for about 20 minutes; then add in the zucchini, the fish and the summer squash.
7. Sprinkle with a little bit of blackening seasoning.
8. Return the Dutch oven to the oven and bake for about 15 minutes
9. Serve and enjoy your dish!

NUTRITION INFORMATION

Calories: 302, Fat: 5.1g, Carbohydrates: 18g, Protein: 34g, Dietary Fiber: 1.1 g

SHRIMP WITH GARLIC

(PREP TIME: 6 MINUTES | COOK TIME: 20 MINUTES | SERVINGS: 3)

INGREDIENTS

- 1 Pound of shrimp
- 1 Tablespoon of olive oil
- 1/8 Teaspoon of chilli flakes
- 3 Tablespoons of chopped garlic
- 2 Tablespoons of milk
- 2 Teaspoons of dried parsley
- 1 and ½ Teaspoons of paprika
- ½ Teaspoon of salt
- ½ Teaspoon of ground black pepper
- 2 Tablespoon of lemon juice

INSTRUCTIONS

1. In a large Dutch oven, mix 1 tablespoon of olive oil, 3 tablespoons of garlic, 1/8 teaspoon of chilli flakes and sauté for about 3 minutes
2. Toss the shrimp into the pan; then add 2 tablespoons of milk
3. Add 2 teaspoons of dried parsley, 1 and ½ teaspoons of paprika, ½ teaspoon of salt
4. Add ½ teaspoon of ground black pepper, and 2 tablespoons of lemon juice.
5. Cover the Dutch oven with a lid and cook for about 15 minutes
6. Transfer the shrimp to a serving platter
7. Serve and enjoy your dish!

NUTRITION INFORMATION

Calories: 210, Fat: 12g, Carbohydrates: 6.3g, Protein: 31.2g, Dietary Fiber: 0.9g

CHAPTER 7: DUTCH OVEN VEGETABLE RECIPES

VEGETABLE DOLMAS

(PREP TIME: 10 MINUTES | COOK TIME: 45 MINUTES | SERVINGS: 5-6)

INGREDIENTS

- 5 Large potatoes
- 3 Large peppers
- 2 Tomatoes
- 3 Medium onions
- 3 Zucchini
- 3 Tablespoons of olive oil
- 1 Pinch of salt
- 1 Pinch of ground black pepper
- 1 Pinch of paprika
- 1 Bunch of flat leaf parsley
- ½ Teaspoon of cinnamon
- Crumbled bread soaked in milk
- 1 Tablespoon of ground flaxseed+ 1 tablespoon of water
- 1 Minced garlic clove

INSTRUCTIONS

4   Start by washing the zucchini, the tomato, the potatoes, the peppers, and the onions

5   Empty your veggies with a tail of a teaspoon or with a knife

6   Place the garlic, the bread crumbs, the parsley and the salt in a large bowl and mix very well

7   Add the flaxseed and the water; then mix very well

8   When your mixture becomes smooth, fill the tomato, the zucchini and the potatoes with the prepared mixture

9   Arrange your stuffed vegetable in a large greased Dutch oven

10 Grate the onion on top of the Dutch oven; then slice the tomatoes in rounds and arrange it around your veggies

11 Season your ingredients with the salt and the ground black pepper; then pour in 1 cup of vegetable stock

12 Cover the Dutch oven with the lid and cook for about 40 to 45 minutes on a medium low heat

13 Transfer your veggies to a serving platter

14 Garnish your veggies with sauce and chopped parsley

15 Serve and enjoy your delicious vegetable dish!

NUTRITION INFORMATION

Calories: 140.3, Fat: 2.1g, Carbohydrates: 13g, Protein: 3.4g, Dietary Fiber: 0.2g

BLACK BEAN CHILLI

(PREP TIME: 6 MINUTES | COOK TIME: 55 MINUTES | SERVINGS: 4)

INGREDIENTS

- 1 and ½ cups of chopped sweet onion
- 1 Large, minced garlic clove
- 1 Seeded and diced jalapeno
- 1 and ½ cups of rinsed and drained; cooked black beans
- ¾ Cup of mild salsa
- 1 Cup of frozen corn kernels
- 2 Teaspoons of chili powder
- 1 Teaspoon of ground cumin
- ½ Teaspoon of kosher salt
- 1 Tablespoon of nutritional yeast
- Diced avocado
- Chopped cilantro
- Sliced green onion

INSTRUCTIONS

1. Spray a large Dutch oven with cooking spray
2. Add the onion and the garlic
3. Chop the jalapeno; then add it in
4. Add the drained and the rinsed black beans
5. Add the salsa; and the corn and stir very well
6. Season with a little bit of salt
7. Close the lid f the Dutch oven and place it on the stove top on a medium high heat and cook for about 50 to 55 minutes
8. When the time is up; unlock the lid and transfer the Chili to a serving platter
9. Top with fresh cilantro
10. Serve and enjoy your bean Chili

NUTRITION INFORMATION

Calories: 239 Fat: 2.4g, Carbohydrates: 18g, Protein: 12g, Dietary Fiber: 0.4g

FAVA BEANS AND LENTIL CURRY

(PREP TIME: 15 MINUTES | COOK TIME: 2 HOURS | SERVINGS: 3-4)

INGREDIENTS

- 1 Pound of dried fava beans
- 2 Teaspoons of baking soda
- ½ Pound of washed and drained red lentils
- 1 Tablespoon of fresh lemon juice
- 1 Teaspoon of ground cumin
- ½ Teaspoon of ground coriander
- 2 Tablespoons of olive oil
- ½ Teaspoon of chilli powder
- 1 Tablespoon of olive oil

INSTRUCTIONS

1. Spray your Dutch Oven with cooking spray; then pour in 4 to 5 cups of water
2. Add the fava beans
3. Cover your Dutch Oven with the lid on top of a stove over a medium high heat and cook for about 55 to 60 minutes; check the water from time to time and you can add more if needed
4. Once your fava beans are perfectly cooked, rinse and drain it; then clean the Dutch Oven and place the back the fava beans with the lentils and pour in 3 cups of water
5. Cover your Dutch Oven with the lid and season with salt and a squeeze of lemon
6. Cook the fava beans and lentils for about 30 minutes
7. Set the ingredients aside to cool for about 10 minutes
8. Squeeze the fresh lemon over the fava beans and the lentils
9. In the meantime; prepare the flavourings and to do that, place a small quantity of fava beans and lentils in a pan over a medium low heat and sprinkle the flavouring
10. Add 2 tablespoons of water and stir
11. Heat your ingredients very well; then season very well with 1 pinch of salt and 1 pinch of ground black pepper
12. Drizzle with the olive oil
13. Serve and enjoy your delicious fava beans!

NUTRITION INFORMATION

Calories: 187 Fat: 6g, Carbohydrates: 22g, Protein: 11g, Dietary Fiber: 0.5g

MUSHROOM RISOTTO

(PREP TIME: 10 MINUTES | COOK TIME: 40 MINUTES | SERVINGS: 3)

INGREDIENTS

- ¾ Oz of dried porcini mushrooms
- 1 Oz of dried shiitake mushrooms
- 5 Cups of low-salt chicken broth
- 2 Tablespoons of coconut oil
- 1 Medium, finely diced yellow onion
- 1 Pinch of Kosher salt
- 1 Pinch of ground black pepper
- 2 Cups of imported Arborio rice
- 1/3 Cup of dry white wine
- 1 and ½ cups of thawed frozen petite peas
- 1 Tablespoon of balsamic vinegar
- 3 Tablespoons of chopped fresh mint
- 1 and ½ teaspoons of chopped fresh thyme

INSTRUCTIONS

1. Place the porcini and the shiitake mushrooms in a large bowl; then pour in 2 cups of boiling water
2. Let the mushrooms soak for about 20 minutes
3. Pat the mushrooms dry with a clean paper towel
4. Transfer the mushrooms to a cutting board
5. Discard any stems of the mushrooms; then set it aside
6. In a Dutch oven, heat the oil then toss in the onion with 1 pinch of salt and 1 pinch of ground black pepper
7. Sauté your ingredients for about 3 minutes
8. Add the rice to the pan and sauté for about 2 minutes
9. Add the mushrooms and cook for about 1 additional minute
10. Add in the wine and stir for about 2 minutes
11. Transfer your ingredients to your Dutch oven; then pour in hot broth or water and close the lid
12. Cook for about 20 to 25 minutes on a medium high heat
13. When the time is up; add in the cooked peas, the vinegar and the half and half
14. Add the thyme and the mint; then season your risotto with 1 pinch of salt and 1 pinch of ground black pepper
15. Transfer your risotto to a serving platter
16. Garnish the risotto with thyme and mint
17. Serve and enjoy your vegetable risotto!

NUTRITION INFORMATION

Calories: 225, Fat: 11g, Carbohydrates: 18.5g, Protein: 8g, Dietary Fiber: 0.8g

VEGETABLE CANNELLONI

(PREP TIME: 9 MINUTES | COOK TIME: 30 MINUTES | SERVINGS: 4)

INGREDIENTS

- 1 Pound of grated pumpkin
- ½ Cup of roughly chopped baby spinach
- 1 Teaspoon of white pepper
- ½ Teaspoon of salt
- 1 Packet of fresh lasagne sheets
- 6 Cups of Tomato puree
- 125 ml of milk
- 3 Tablespoons of chopped parsley

INSTRUCTIONS

1. Place a large Dutch oven over a medium high heat; then pour in about 1/3 of the bottle of the passata into the bottom
2. In a large bowl; mix altogether the baby spinach, the pumpkin, the white pepper and the salt
3. Make the shape of sausage from the mixture to the end of the pasta
4. Place the pasta cannelloni in the bottom of your Dutch oven right over the top of the passata
5. Pour the passata over the sheets of cannelloni and the evaporated milk
6. Cover the Dutch oven with a lid and cook for about 30 minutes on a medium heat
7. When the time is up; remove the Dutch oven from the heat and transfer the cannelloni to a serving platter
8. Sprinkle the cannelloni with 1 pinch of ground black pepper and fresh parsley
9. Serve and enjoy your delicious vegetable cannelloni!

NUTRITION INFORMATION

Calories: 330, Fat: 12g, Carbohydrates: 19g, Protein: 18.9g, Dietary Fiber: 1.2g

CHAPTER 8: DUTCH OVEN BREAD RECIPES

CINNAMON BREAD

(PREP TIME: 10 MINUTES | COOK TIME: 45 MINUTES | SERVINGS: 7)

INGREDIENTS

- 1 and ½ cups of flour
- ¾ Teaspoon of baking soda
- ½ Teaspoon of baking powder
- ¼ Teaspoon of salt
- 1 Teaspoon of cinnamon
- ½ Teaspoon of ground all spice
- 4Tbsp of butter
- 2 Large organic eggs
- 1 Cup of avocado puree
- ½ Cup of heavy cream
- ½ Tbsp of grated lemon zest

INSTRUCTIONS

1. Preheat your oven to 340° F and place a 6-quart Dutch oven in it to heat for at least 30 minutes
2. In a deep bowl, combine all together the flour, the baking powder, the salt, the lemon zest, the all spice and the cinnamon and mix very well.
3. Pour the butter in a bowl and with a hand mixer beat it until it becomes soft and very smooth.
4. Add in the eggs and the avocado puree then carry on mixing the ingredients
5. Add your dry mixture and the heavy cream into your batter and Mix it very well until it is very well combined.
6. Remove the Dutch oven from the oven and line it with a baking paper
7. Grease the Dutch oven with a little bit of oil; then pour in the batter and cover it with the lid
8. Place the Dutch oven back in the oven and bake for about 45 minutes at a temperature of 400° F
9. Remove the Dutch oven from the oven and set it aside to cool for 5 minutes
10. Slice the bread; then serve and enjoy it!

NUTRITION INFORMATION

Calories: 174, Fat: 17g, Carbohydrates: 5g, Protein: 4.8g, Dietary Fiber: 1.9g

CASHEW BREAD

(PREP TIME: 7 MINUTES | COOK TIME: 50 MINUTES | SERVINGS: 5)

INGREDIENTS

- 2Tablespoons of vegetable oil
- 2 and ½ cups of whole raw cashews
- 7 Tablespoons of flour
- 8 Beaten large eggs
- ½ Cup of milk
- 4 Teaspoons of apple cider vinegar
- 4 teaspoons of baking powder
- 1 Teaspoon of salt

INSTRUCTIONS

1. Put a 6- quart Dutch oven in the oven at a temperature of 325° F about ½ hour before baking the bread
2. Mix the flour, the cashews, the eggs, the milk, the apple cider vinegar, the salt and the baking powder and process the mixture for around 30 to 40 seconds
3. Once the mixture becomes very thick, add 1 to 2 tbsp of water and process again until the mixture becomes smooth
4. Remove the Dutch oven from the oven and line it with a parchment paper; then grease with a little bit of oil
5. Pour the batter into the Dutch oven and cover with a lid
6. Place the Dutch oven in the preheated oven and bake for about 45 to 50 minutes
7. Once the bread gets a golden brown color, remove the Dutch oven from the oven and discard it from the parchment paper.
8. Slice the bread; serve and enjoy it mesmerizing taste!

NUTRITION INFORMATION

Calories: 201.5, Fat: 15.6g, Carbohydrates: 12.3g, Protein: 5.8g, Dietary Fiber: 1.4g

SESAME SEEDS BREAD

(PREP TIME: 10 MINUTES | COOK TIME: 60 MINUTES | SERVINGS: 4)

INGREDIENTS

- 1 Cup of almond flour
- ¼ Cup of sesame seeds
- ½ Cup of golden flaxseed meal
- ½ Cup of pumpkin seeds
- 1 Cup of sunflower seeds
- 2 Tbsp of chia seeds
- ¼ Cup of water
- 1and ¼ teaspoon of salt
- 5 Beaten eggs
- 2 Tbsp of sesame seeds to sprinkle it on the top of batter

INSTRUCTIONS

1. Preheat your oven to around 350° F and line a 6-quart Dutch oven with parchment paper.
2. Place the Dutch oven in the oven about ½ hour before baking the bread
3. In a deep and large bowl; combine all together the almond meal, the sesame seeds, the flaxseed meal, the pumpkin seeds, the sunflower seeds, and the chia seeds
4. Add the salt and mix very well.
5. Pour in the water and the eggs all at once, and stir your ingredients very well until you obtain a smooth batter
6. Remove the Dutch oven from the oven; then pour the batter into it already and sprinkle with 1 pinch of sesame seeds on top of your bread
7. Cover the Dutch oven with the lid and place it in the preheated oven
8. Bake the bread for around 55 to 60 minutes
9. Remove the Dutch oven from the oven and discard it from the parchment paper
10. Slice the bread into pieces, then serve and enjoy it!

NUTRITION INFORMATION

Calories: 144.7, Fat: 9.8g, Carbohydrates: 11.5g, Protein: 3.8g, Dietary Fiber: 1.2g

CHAPTER 9: DUTCH OVEN DESSERT RECIPES

CHOCOLATE BROWNIES

(PREP TIME: 10 MINUTES | COOK TIME: 35 MINUTES | SERVINGS: 12)

INGREDIENTS

- ½ Cup of butter
- ¼ Cup of olive oil
- ¾ Cup of raw organic honey
- ½ of mashed banana
- 1 Tablespoon of vanilla extract
- 1 Cup of all purpose flour
- ¼ Cup of cacao powder
- 1 Teaspoon of baking soda
- ¼ Teaspoon of salt
- 4 Oz of sugar-free chocolate chips
- 4 Oz of chopped walnuts

INSTRUCTIONS

1. Preheat your oven to a temperature of about 350° F.
2. Place a 6-quart Dutch oven in the oven and let heat for about 30 minutes
3. Mix altogether the butter with the olive oil
4. Add the honey; then egg; the vanilla extract
5. Into another bowl; mix altogether the flour; the honey
6. Crack in the egg and the vanilla extract into a small bowl.
7. In another small bowl; mix the flour with the cacao powder; the baking soda and the salt
8. Add the dry ingredients to the wet ingredients; then stir very well
9. Add in the chocolate chips and the chopped walnuts
10. Remove the Dutch oven from the oven and pour the batter in it
11. Cover the Dutch oven with a lid and place it back in the oven; bake for about 35 minutes at a temperature of 350° F
12. Remove the Dutch oven from the oven and let cool for 5 minutes into 12 squares
13. Serve and enjoy your delicious brownies

NUTRITION INFORMATION

Calories: 205.3, Fat: 17.5g, Carbohydrates: 11.7g, Protein: 5 g, Dietary Fiber: 0.8g

PEACH COBBLER

(PREP TIME: 15 MINUTES | COOK TIME: 25 MINUTES | SERVINGS: 8)

INGREDIENTS

- 8 Cups of fresh sliced peaches
- 2 Cups of sugar
- 4 Tablespoons of all-purpose flour
- ½ Teaspoon of ground nutmeg
- 1 Teaspoon of Vanilla extract
- 1/3 Cup of Butter
- Pastry for double-crust pie
- 1 Cup of Vanilla ice cream

INSTRUCTIONS

1. Combine the peaches with the sugar, the flour, and the nutmeg in a large Dutch oven; then set aside until a syrup forms.

2. Bring the peach mixture to a boil; then reduce the heat to low, and cook your ingredients for about 10 minutes or until it becomes tender.

3. Remove the Dutch oven from the heat; then add in the vanilla and the butter and make sure to stir until the butter melts

4. Roll half the pastry into a thickness of ½ inch over a floured surface; then cut the pastry into squares of 8 inches

5. Clean the Dutch oven and lightly grease it with oil or butter

6. Spoon half the quantity of the peaches into your Dutch oven

7. Top the peaches with the pastry and cover the Dutch oven with the lid

8. Place the Dutch oven in the preheated oven and bake for about 15 minutes at a temperature of 475° F

9. Roll the remaining pastry to a thickness of 1/8 inch; then cut it into strips

10. Remove the Dutch oven from the oven and arrange the pastry strips on top; then cover with a lid and return it to the oven

11. Bake for about 15 additional minutes

12. Spoon the cobbler into bowls or cups; then serve and enjoy your dessert!

NUTRITION INFORMATION

Calories: 250, Fat: 14g, Carbohydrates: 25g, Protein: 5.1 g, Dietary Fiber: 0.1g

CHOCOLATE CAKE

(PREP TIME: 10 MINUTES | COOK TIME: 35 MINUTES | SERVINGS: 6)

INGREDIENTS

FOR THE WET INGREDIENTS

- ¼ Cup olive oil
- 3 Large eggs
- ¼ Cup maple syrup, pure
- 1 Cup orange juice, freshly squeezed
- 1 Large orange, zest
- ¼ Cup milk

FOR THE CHOCOLATE GLAZE

- 4 Oz chocolate bar

FOR THE DRY INGREDIENTS

- 2 Cups all purpose flour
- 1 Pinch salt
- 1 tsp baking soda

FOR THE GARNISH

- 1 orange, only zest

INSTRUCTIONS

1. Preheat an oven to about 350° F; then place a 6-quart Dutch oven in it and let heat for about 30 minutes
2. Combine the flour with the salt and baking soda in a large mixing bowl and mix
3. Now, combine the maple syrup with the eggs, the orange juice and the milk in a separate bowl and add the oil to the mixture
4. Whisk the wet ingredients very well; then add the dry ingredients you have placed in a separate bowl to the wet ingredients and combine everything together
5. Line your Dutch oven with a parchment paper and pour the batter in it
6. Cover the Dutch oven with its lid and place it in the oven
7. Bake the cake for about 40 minutes
8. Remove the Dutch oven from the oven and set it aside to cool for about 5 minutes; in the meantime, make the dark chocolate glaze by adding the dark chocolate bar by bringing a pot to a boil; then toss the chocolate into a small bowl and place the bowl in the water (The level of the water shouldn't be elevated so that it won't penetrate into the chocolate and ruin it) stir from time to time until the chocolate becomes smooth
9. Pour the batter over the cake and evenly spread it on top
10. Top with the orange zest; then slice the cake
11. Serve and enjoy your delicious cake!

NUTRITION INFORMATION

Calories: 238, Fat: 11.8, Carbohydrates: 17g, Protein: 10.4g, Dietary Fiber: 2.7g

CONCLUSION

Of all cookware equipments, Dutch oven makes one of its own thanks to its versatility and great ease of use. And that is why Dutch ovens has become one of the most favourite and addictive cooking experiences.

Not only you can make soups and stews in a Dutch oven, but you can also make desserts, sweets and even breads. In a few words, we can say that Dutch ovens are the best investment you can bring to your kitchen and that can help you in your special occasions.

So when you believe you are ready to start this enjoyable Dutch oven cooking experience, this book is a great place to start from with sumptuous recipes that will inspire you to cook some of your favourite recipes.

And what is more pleasant about the Dutch oven is that you can use it to cook indoors or outdoors, you can also take this cookware with you wherever you go because it fits any backpack and you can use it in camps while enjoying with your friends.

Dutch ovens garnered a great popularity all over world and whether you are new to using the Dutch oven or you are a professional, this cookware will bring the nostalgic taste of the past to your dish and will help you enjoy cooking more.

So if you are not familiar with the Dutch oven, this cookbook will make a great start for you. Through this book, I have tried to help you understand more the function of the Dutch oven, the benefits of Dutch oven, its use, tips in addition to a large array of delicious recipes you will greatly enjoy.

And if you are questioning yourself why you should use a Dutch oven instead of using any other cookware, you will find all the answers you are looking for in this cookbook. And if you are looking for meat recipes, fish recipes, bread recipes and even dessert recipes; then you have come to the right place and you have picked the right book.

The recipes in this book are healthy and delicious; besides, you will find a recipe for that is suitable with each of you. Whether you are a vegetarian or you love proteins, this book includes a wide variety of recipes that will satisfy all tastes.

THANKS FOR READING OUR BOOK

I am happy to share with you this Dutch oven cookbook and I take pride in offering you a large array of recipes that you will love and enjoy with healthy ingredients. I hope that you benefit from each of our recipes and I am certain that you will like all the recipes we have offered you.

Don't hesitate to try our creative and easy-to make recipes and remember that I have put my heart to come up with delicious meals for you. If you like my recipes; you can share it with your acquaintances and friends. I need your encouragement to continue writing more books that you will enjoy reading!

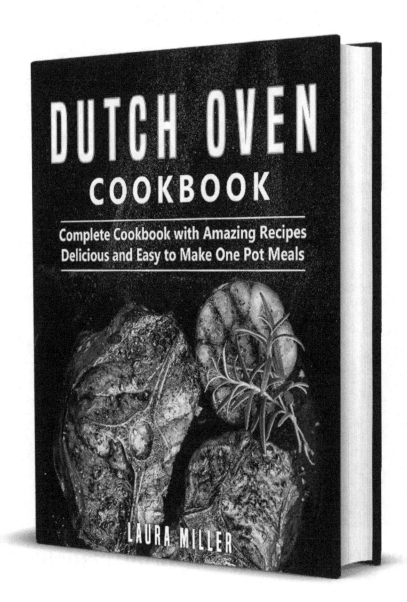

My Books

https://www.amazon.com/dp/1730788580

Legal Notice: *ISBN: 9781091165205*

Disclaimer Notice:

Please note the information contained in this document is for educational and entertainment purposes only. Every attempt has been made to provide accurate, up to date and reliable complete information. No warranties of any kind are expressed or implied. Readers acknowledge that the author is not engaging in the rendering of legal, financial, medical or professional advice. By reading this document, the reader agrees that under no circumstances are we responsible for any losses, direct or indirect, which are incurred as a result of the use of information contained within this document, including, but not limited to, — errors, omissions, or inaccuracies.